GW00984157

Loving You

Discover Your True Inner Self

Michelle Carter

BALBOA
PRESS

A DIVISION OF HAY HOUSE

Balboa Press books may be ordered through booksellers or by contacting:

Balboa Press
A Division of Hay House
1663 Liberty Drive
Bloomington, IN 47403
www.balboapress.com
1 (877) 407-4847

Because of the dynamic nature of the Internet, any web addresses or
links contained in this book may have changed since publication and
may no longer be valid. The views expressed in this work are solely those
of the author and do not necessarily reflect the views of the publisher,
and the publisher hereby disclaims any responsibility for them.

The author of this book does not dispense medical advice or prescribe
the use of any technique as a form of treatment for physical, emotional,
or medical problems without the advice of a physician, either directly
or indirectly. The intent of the author is only to offer information
of a general nature to help you in your quest for emotional and
spiritual well-being. In the event you use any of the information in
this book for yourself, which is your constitutional right, the author
and the publisher assume no responsibility for your actions.

Any people depicted in stock imagery provided by Thinkstock are
models, and such images are being used for illustrative purposes only.
Certain stock imagery © Thinkstock.

Printed in the United States of America.

ISBN: 978-1-4525-2278-4 (sc)
ISBN: 978-1-4525-2279-1 (e)

Balboa Press rev. date: 10/02/2014

Contents

Prefix and About the Author

Michelle Carter is an International Divine Energy Channel, the founder of Pure Love Transmissions and has become famous for her powerful Energy Releases.

With the ability to connect direct to Divine Energies and channel very powerful energy transmissions, Michelle changes the lives of those who work with her, remotely, through her on-line groups and through listening to her audios.

Her powerful releasing energy work helps people all over the world release blocks in their lives that are stopping them from living the life of their dreams.

Michelle Carter's vision is a life where people spontaneously smile for no reason, with love overflowing to all they meet, and life for everyone is full of joy, happiness and laughter!

Michelle believes this life is possible through energy work and has found *releasing unwanted energy* and *filling with love* is a very powerful way to change your life.

Loving You has been 'infused and filled with Divine Energies so that just holding or reading this book will release unwanted energies from you and raise your vibration, helping you to feel good. Loving You has been compiled with Love & Light to help anyone who is seeking to find a better life find inner peace and your True You!

It was never a dream or ambition of mine to be an author and I've never considered myself as a writer. In fact, I never liked writing at school, and used to dread having to write essays and stories. So why am I writing this book?

Well, having said that I used to hate writing at school, I have found myself writing advice emails to friends, which then moved on to a blog and a closed facebook group, which has now developed into my Membership site. In these emails, posts and articles, I actually found it easy to write, as I was expressing ideas and views which I strongly believed in and which I thought could, and would help others. I was inspired to have my own vision of what I would like life to be like, which I will share with you below:-

- ♥ My vision is a life where people spontaneously smile for no reason!
- ♥ Where random acts of kindness, just happen because people are so full of love!
- ♥ That their love just overflows into everyone they meet, and life for everyone is full of joy, happiness and laughter!
- ♥ I believe this is possible through energy work and have found releasing unwanted energy and filling with love is a very powerful way to change your life.

So from this came the 'calling' to put all my ideas together into a book. Now I do tend to have a lot of ideas, that can randomly appear into my thoughts, so I decided to prioritize my thoughts and to write a book about Love & Loving Ourselves, as it does appear to be lacking so much in our lives today, and this lack is being shown over and over again in my energy work, to be the main cause of unhappiness, illness and dis-harmony in the world.

I do truly believe that we would all feel so much better, happier, more peaceful and *full of love*, if we did have more 'Love & Loving of Ourselves' in our lives!

Now because I don't consider myself to be an author, it is possible that I may have ignored some of the many rules there are around grammar and writing, but when we stop and think about this, it is just a matter of preference rather than life or death! So maybe it is time for us all to lighten up on the rules and regulations that surround us and control our lives.

In fact, having so much pointless red tape, rules, beliefs, programming and following the crowd without any thought as to why or *is it right for me?*, are the exact reasons why the world and everyone (well most of us!) are feeling so totally disconnected from our true selves and feeling unhappy, unloved, undeserving and ... I won't go on, but I'm sure you all have your own list of emotions you would rather not have!

So Welcome!
As getting rid of all these unwanted emotions and:

Feeling loved,
Feeling happy,
Feeling deserving,
Feeling proud of you, and
Feeling love for yourself – & 'Loving You' - just as you are!

Yes! I did say, ***just as you are,*** - Is what this book is all about.

Why do we Feel Unloved and Unable to Love Ourselves?

To find a way to change our current world, into a happier, more loving place to live, a good question to ask might be:-
'Why do so many of us feel unloved and unable to openly love ourselves?'

If you are thinking that doesn't apply to me, I do love myself, then you may be in for a little surprise later on in the book, with an amazing and so powerful exercise I have. *(For the impatient Aries and others amongst you, (no judgment as that includes me!) then you can go straight to the Mirror Exercise, and then come back here later.)*

But, the thought has come into my head whilst typing this; why would you be reading this book if you totally believed you did Love Yourself? Silly question, as you've all disappeared off to do the mirror exercise!

So welcome back, and let's crack on with the question of:-

Why Love & Self-Love is so lacking in the world today?

Well here are some answers that I came up with, you can probably think of several more:-

- ♥ It's just not the done thing to like yourself!
- ♥ It's considered to be big headed to like yourself and to openly admit this in public.
- ♥ The same applies for anything you have done and achieved.
- ♥ How often do you hear someone say I did 'xyz' and I'm really proud of it?
- ♥ Are we even allowed to be proud of our achievements?
- ♥ It's considered the done thing to put yourself down, list all your faults, from a big nose to fat thighs, and everything in between!
- ♥ Life is so busy that people don't have time to be nice.
- ♥ Comparison is the 'in thing'- from keeping up with the Jones's, to having to have the ideal supermodel figure, face, image, earn the most money and have the newest and best car, home, etc.

So when we don't live up to these high standards, we just assume we are not as good as others and decide that everything about us and our lives is no good and that we are no good!

We are programmed from birth that you have to fit into the 'social standard' person, job, family etc. Our lives are planned out, that we go to school, college/university, get a well paid job, get married, have 2.2 children, they leave home, we retire, then we die! You will not deviate from this preset plan, you will not pass go and collect £200! (Sorry bit of monopoly programming slipping in there, and I didn't even play it that much!)

So if you're not successful, rich, supermodel figure etc then you are a failure! That is what most of us believe on some level - Now how *sad* is that!

How many of us had parents / carers/ teachers who said you can study whatever you like? You can do any job you want? You can do whatever you want with your life that makes you happy, because it is ***your life!***

Well, I haven't met anyone yet who did, *(except my daughters, who when I read this to them, said 'you do Mummy!' How sweet!)* So I'm assuming that, especially as you're reading this book, that your parents didn't say any of those wonderful things to you, and that if they had, then you wouldn't be reading this book!

In fact, I would go as far as to say, that we were programmed from birth, by parents, carers, teachers, educational systems, governments and the media to do anything *except* what makes us happy!

Why does the whole world, (or most of it) want us to be *unhappy*? What is the point of living a life of unhappiness? Is that Living? Or is that just existing?

What is wrong with the concept that *life is for enjoying!* Wow! Sorry, what was that? No one ever told me that!

Well actually that isn't entirely true for me, I can distinctly remember a dance partner saying to me at a dance, 'For goodness sake Michelle, Lighten Up! Life is for enjoying, you know!' My life was pretty grim at the time! And I can remember thinking about this statement, and then thinking some more, and wondering, 'Have I ever been happy'? I wasn't happy as a child. Random strangers would often say to me as a 4-5 year old and even more as I got older, 'Smile, it might never happen!' or 'Don't look so serious, you're only a child!'

But on deeper reflection, I could remember being happy when I was *enjoying* (funny, it's that word again!) various sports and water sports as a teenager. When I was doing these activities, I felt I was a different person to the Michelle that my friends and family knew.

Now does that sound familiar? Being more than one person to fit in with your situation! Why can't we just **be me?** And have life accept us 'just as we are?'

So what does all of this mean? That everything and everyone around us has influenced who *we are*, and the person who's probably had the least input into who *we are*, is ourselves!

So it is time... **We claimed our lives back!**

It is time, we allowed ourselves to *be who we want to be* and to *do what we want to do!*

So that is exactly what we are going to do... Right now.

Buckle your seats belts, adjust your head rest, We're going to **blow your mind open!** And all you need to do is *enjoy!*

I Can't Do This, It's Just Not Me!

I hadn't intended this chapter to be next, but then when I was thinking about the book in general I decided:-

Let's take the bull by the horns and get rid of this one right now!

Firstly, do you want to be able to do this?

Would you like your life to be better than it is now? And the answer to that must be *yes* or you wouldn't be reading this book!

So, if you do want to do this, then your thoughts and resistance must be related to thinking you can't do it, you might fail, you're not good enough or you're just not the type of person to do this sort of stuff, even though you don't yet know what sort of stuff that might be.

Time for some ***uplifting questions:***

What if it was really easy?
What if it was fun?
What if I could do it?
What if it could change my life for the better, forever?
What if I chose to just be open minded and give it a go?
What is the worst thing that could happen? *(Probably that you don't even try!)*

So how about you just keep reading the next paragraph, without any thoughts or judgments.

I release all resistance, thoughts, beliefs & emotions you have to:-
Change,
Believing you can't change,
Thinking this is all weird and you don't do weird stuff,
Thinking you can't or shouldn't do it,
Thinking you will fail,
Thinking you will give up,
Thinking it won't work for you,
Any fears that it will work and then you will be different,
Thinking what will the neighbours think,
And any other beliefs, feelings, emotions, patterns, programming and all low vibrations and energy you may have about this book and your intentions towards it and in relation to improving your life and allowing You to Be You!

Well, that wasn't too difficult or weird was it?

I'm trusting that has released all your reasons and resistance to not actively choosing to read and do anything suggested in this book, but just in case it hasn't fully worked, (as I can't tune into the energies of who's going to read this book in the future - or maybe I can and that is why I feel some of you are not fully on board)

Then here is another easy to read paragraph for you.

I release all energies, including all fears from the whole of my mind, body, spirit and energy field, relating to thinking:-
I can't do this, it's just not me, I always fail or give up, none of these books ever work anyway, it's just words and words can't change me, nothing ever works for me, I've tried everything and I just can't change, I can't just be open minded and any other energies and low vibrations relating to failure,

I release all these vibrations and energies now from this moment of now and from all past and future moments of now.

Ok, so I am now trusting that you are feeling open minded enough to carry on!

Well done! That was a pretty major achievement for some of you, so give yourselves a pat on the back!
(*Now that is a funny expression, such a hard thing to actually do!*)

A few little notes for you before we continue:-

Acknowledging your achievements is good!
Self praise is good!
Humour is Awesome!
Feeling Happy is Awesome!

Being too serious is not good.
Being tough and hard on yourself is not nice, would you be unkind to your best friend? Usually no, so then don't be unkind to yourself!
(*See the chapter on Do You Really Expect Me to Love Myself? Tip: answer is yes!*)

So what's next I ask myself?

Learning how to feel
How can I just enjoy my life?
Releasing your resistance to being able to just enjoy my life
You don't really expect me to *love myself*?
The mirror exercise!
What is true, unconditional love?

And I really didn't know the answer, so I thought I'd sleep on it and see if some amazing inspiration popped into my head, which it did… So next is Diamonds!

Diamonds you are all thinking, has she gone totally mad, what have diamonds got to do with any of the above?

Well, keep reading and you will find out!

Diamonds – Your True Inner Self

I would like to use diamonds in a visual way to explain more easily about layers of energy and how they affect our lives. Just consider all feelings, emotions, beliefs, genetic patterns, programming etc to be layers of energy.

If you imagine we are all a shining, bright diamond when we are born. Our true selves shining out to the whole world, and saying 'I'm such a shining, bright light, look at me, see how I sparkle! I am awesome, I love being this pure, I love being me!'

And then… Life happens!

We hear people argue, we smell exhaust fumes, are parents feel stressed with life, we go to school, watch TV, friends upset us, we become ill, we eat junk food, we absorb all the negative energies and programming all around us and so on!

All of this has an effect on our beautiful shining, bright diamond and it gets wrapped in pieces of tissue paper, to protect it from all the low and unwanted energies we are living in.

And as life goes on more and more pieces of tissue paper get wrapped around the diamond, so the diamond is no longer visible and could just be a rock. No Sparkle.

Major life upsets happen and the diamond gets wrapped in black tissue paper, so now we can't see how many layers of tissue paper are underneath and we feel really disconnected from our true 'diamond' self.

We no longer know or feel we are a diamond and we definitely no longer think 'I am awesome, I sparkle, I love being me!'

Instead we think, 'Life is so hard, I'm so rubbish, I hate my body, and so on, *(that's more than enough negatives to type and read!)*

We may decide to take action, healing, hypnosis etc and this changes a layer of tissue paper to a pretty pink with loving hearts all over it, so it looks pretty to look at, but it doesn't stop the energies of the layers of tissue paper underneath from effecting us, so we feel we have made some progress but still don't feel we are our 'true diamond self'.

However, we don't just have one diamond, we have 3 diamonds! Wow 3, now that is a lot of layers! We have a diamond in our minds, relating to all our thoughts and beliefs, another in our hearts for all our feelings and emotions and the third is in our solar plexus connecting us to our True Divine Connection through our 'gut feelings'.

The diamond we are going to work with for this book is our Feeling Diamond. Some of you may 'feel' it in your hearts and some in your solar plexus or 'gut feeling', you can use either or both, which ever feels easiest and strongest for you.

And... If you haven't already guessed, all our diamonds get wrapped in layers of tissue paper, from all our collected emotions, hurts, pains and trauma to do with love, or should I say lack of love. So every time you have felt a major emotion of being unloved, rejected, unwanted and undeserving of love, then a layer has been wrapped around your heart to protect it from further hurts.

Now, I would like to teach you all how to 'feel' from your heart or gut, but chances are that it is so wrapped in layers of protection that you could well struggle to 'feel', especially those of you who have lots and lots of layers of protection - and don't despair if you feel or know that this is you, because it was once the case for me, so there is hope for you!

And, I guess that actually makes the next chapter rather easy to decide on! Removing Heart Barriers. *(Which is the name generally given to all your layers of protection, or tissue paper in our diamond example above.)*

As, I'm sure you will all appreciate, trying to feel something that has layers of protection around it is going to be a lot harder than trying to feel with an open heart and a shining, bright diamond in your heart.

So it's definitely time to get rid of all those nasty, unwanted layers of old, stuck emotions from around your beautiful loving heart!

Releasing Your Heart Barriers

Right! Getting rid of unwanted layers of energy and protection around our heart - sounds a bit nasty! How on earth are we going to do this!

Time for more questions.
Which layers should we remove first?
And how are we going to remove them anyway?

Well, as this book is about Loving You and feeling love, we are going to remove, *(from now on called 'releasing')*, the layers from our heart barriers. This will allow us to FEEL our true self, although with all the other layers we may still not see or know that we are a diamond yet!

When we start to release layers from around our 'Feeling Diamond', we will become closer to our 'true self". Then, when we have taken away enough black layers of tissue paper, we will see and recognise that we **are** a diamond, wrapped in tissue paper, and not a rock! The more layers we release the more we connect with our true, shining, bright diamond self.

Each person has their own specific layers of tissue paper, depending on their life challenges and stored emotions etc, and will need to release all energies relating to these. The layers don't need to be released in any order, but starting with the big black ones will give the biggest impact! Then it's just a question of patiently finding and releasing all of the others, realising that it is a journey to uncovering *your own sparkling, bright diamond*.

When you see you are a diamond, then the process and releasing gets so much easier and you start to love yourself, **just as you are!** (*With a little help from the remaining chapters!*)

First let's just read another release to get rid of any thoughts, emotions and beliefs that may have come up whilst reading any of the above, so just read and allow.

'I ask that all energies and barriers that are stopping you from feeling, being open to feel, being open to just try and see what happens are released from you now.'

So now it is time to . . . . Learn how to FEEL! Yes!!!!! This is soooo exciting!

Learning How
to FEEL

Some of you may be thinking 'thanks but I already know how to feel, and for some of you that will be true, but for many of you, what you consider to be 'feeling' is actually 'thinking'!!

Now this may sound a little confusing, so just go with it and we'll do a physical feeling exercise afterwards to 'feel' the difference between thinking and feeling!

But first of all, I think it would be beneficial to experience the feeling of feeling! (*sorry this sounds so confusing!*)

Think of a very happy event, someone you love or something that makes you happy, and then 'feel' where you feel that sensation, and really feel what it feels like - light, happy, warm, good!

So where did you feel the feeling? In your heart or in your gut? This is the place you need to go to, to experience a real feeling.

If you want a comparison then you can 'feel' an unhappy, sad or upsetting emotion, but if you do this then go back to the good emotion - you don't want to carry on your day in anything other than a good, happy feeling!

Now back to feeling versus thinking!

When we 'feel' something we can either 'feel' the 'feeling' or we can 'feel' the thought! Most people tend to live in their heads, especially with all the programming and layers of tissue paper or rubbish wrapped around our hearts and 'Feeling Diamond'.

So ...... The question is:-
Are you 'feeling' your real 'feeling' or
Are you 'feeling' your 'thought'?

So before you spend too much time trying to think about that! Let's do a 'feel' example!

Let's try something that everyone can relate to. Pick something you love to do that makes you feel good, or a memory that instantly makes you feel good. Now think in your head about that issue or memory and notice how you feel and where you feel this.

Now clear that feeling, but remember it, and now imagine you are actually doing the thing you love or relive the memory with all the details, in colour with all the details and emotions that go with this. Close your eyes and live the moment, you are now doing the thing chose that you love, now how do you feel and where is this feeling?

What most of us do, when we think we are feeling, is we analyze our thoughts and then feel these thoughts, which gives a completely different feeling to feeling what is in your heart or gut when you are imaging or really feeling the feeling. It has been proved that our minds and bodies don't actually know the difference between something we imagine and the real thing, so imagining is so much more powerful than just thinking about something.

As being able to 'feel' in this way, is what this book is about and is the basis of Loving You, then I think we need to take another example, to make sure you have all 'really felt it' and understand the difference.

Imagine you are unhappy in your job so you apply for new jobs. You get offered two jobs at the same time and you have to make a decision about which job to accept.

So normally, we would either ask someone what they think! Or make a list of pros and cons and try and decide from that list, ie think which list is most in our favour, or just do what our friend said to do!

Now what if you did this instead:-

Imagine yourself arriving at work for job 1, and working there for the day. Drop into your feeling place, and feel what it would be like to work there. Then do the same for job 2. Which job had the better feeling?

Another way to do this, is to feel which is the best job for you at this moment of time?

To do this you drop into your feeling place, and ask 'which job is best for me at this moment in time, job 1 - FEEL, or job 2 - FEEL.

What feelings did you get for each job?

Or you could try this method, ask a 'yes or no' question, 'Is job 1 the best job for me at this moment of time?' Yes / No

& to confirm, 'Is job 2 the best job for me at this moment of time?' Yes / No

Now how this feeling works for each of you will be different, because we are all amazing, unique individuals!

When I do this feeling method, I will feel either good, light and have a 'this is right for me' type of feeling or a no, bad, sinking, 'don't go there' type of feeling.

With the Yes/No type of question, I will get a physical nod or shake of my head, which can be quite visible at times! (*So I do choose when & where I do this! It's one thing having people thinking you're slightly crazy, but I don't want to get locked up!*)

So that is how you really FEEL. Well done on experiencing FEELING!

Once you have mastered this skill of feeling, then you can ask yourself all sorts of questions and feel the answers! The more you practice it the easier it becomes! This is a totally awesome tool to have and it's totally Free, totally yours and there 24/7!

Just in case you didn't get good results with the above, then here is a release for you. Read this release and try the above exercises again.

If you still can't feel it then take a break, read the release again, have another break and come back to the exercises another day.

Remember, **You can do this**! *(As long as you don't give up!)*

'I release all feelings, thoughts & emotions that are preventing me from having the experience 'of feeling' that I desire in the above exercise.
I release any other reasons & energies that may be stopping me from having a 'gut feeling' in either my heart or gut.
I allow myself to be open to having whatever feelings I have.
I trust that 'I can feel' and this is just a skill that can be learnt
I desire to learn to 'Feel' so I am willing to keep going until it works for me.'

So now we have learnt how to 'Feel', let's find out what exactly it is we want to feel!

True, unconditional love?

What is True, Unconditional Love?

Well, I believe this is a very good question! And I also believe that most of us don't know the answer, as we have never experienced it!

Love is a **feeling!**
Being loved is a **feeling!**
Unconditional love is a **feeling!**

Unconditional love is NOT lust, fancying someone, hero worshiping someone or even the feeling we have when we first fall in love with someone!

So what is it?

It is loving someone *'Just the way they are'*

- with no conditions or judgments, not wanting to change anything about them or anything they do, but just wanting them to be - alive - and with you. Sound weird? Ever had that feeling with anyone? Well neither had I until . .. . .

I was seriously ill and spent months on end, stuck in bed, too weak and ill to get up, too ill to look after my two daughters and feeling totally useless and thinking and feeling what exactly was the point of me being alive if I couldn't do anything?!!

My daughters were very supportive and loving towards me during this time, which was much appreciated, as I felt they were the only ones who really cared whether I lived or died! *(and that probably wasn't true at all, but it was how I felt at that time!)* My daughters would regularly tell me that they loved me and that I was 'The Best Mum in the World!'

On one of my really low days, I can remember thinking, 'how can they say that?' They can't really mean it, I'm totally useless, I can't look after them, how can they think I'm 'The Best Mum in the World?', they must be just saying it to make me feel good! But, then I knew and 'felt' that they did mean it. So, with nothing else to do, or nothing else that I could do! I started to think and wonder why they truly did think and believe I was 'The Best Mum in the World', when I was too ill to look after them.

The answer I came up with, was that they 'felt I loved them', they 'loved the feeling that I loved them', and they were really scared that I might get so ill that I would die, so they kept telling me how much they loved me and that I was 'The Best Mum in the World', because they wanted me -alive!

Yes, that was it, they just wanted me to be alive! They really would desire for me to be well and happy, of course, but they loved me '**Just as I Was**' and that was enough!

So, that is my explanation of the 'Feeling of Unconditional Love'.

When someone loves you, just as you are! Nothing added, nothing taken away! Just Alive!!

Wow - Yes!

Now can you imagine 'Loving Yourself - Just as You Are Now?'

Nothing added, nothing taken away, not richer, or smarted, or thinner, or more successful, or .. .. But *Just as You Are Now.*

No!

Neither could I! Neither did I!

I needed to be well at least to love myself, and then I needed to have lost the weight I'd put on whilst being ill, and I needed to get fit again, and be financially independent and able to earn enough money to have a good lifestyle, and so on.....! Sound familiar?

Well **now** I do love myself - Just the way I am now!

And read on to find out how I did it!!

You don't really expect me to LOVE MYSELF?

Well, phrased like that then no! I don't particularly like the word 'expect' but it was what came into my head as something we might think or say to ourselves, so I've gone with it!

But . . . . I do believe you CAN Love Yourself and I do believe you deserve to be loved, just as you are.

Now some of you may be thinking how can I say that when I don't know you and what you've done, and you could well be thinking of all the bad things that you think you may have done that would cause you not to deserve to be loved, but the truth is, if you are reading this book then you do deserve to be loved.

Most of us have done our best with the layers we had covering our diamond and if you are here then you are desiring to move forwards, so sometimes when I'm giving myself a hard time, I ask myself - 'well would anyone else have done it that much better?' and even if they would have, we still did the best we could, which is all we can do in each moment.

And besides all that, loving is about *not judging*! You can love someone and still disapprove of their behaviour or actions. Loving is accepting what is and being willing to help if needed.

I love my daughters, unconditionally, just as they are, but I can still disapprove of any unloving behaviour and do my best to guide them to see the effect that has on others around them.

So, back to where we were!

I believe you CAN love yourself and I believe you deserve to be loved, Just as you are!

Now some of you, with very low self esteem are going to be challenged with these exercises, *(as I was when I first did them)* so take you time, be kind to yourself and love yourself!

So first tip on how to love yourself. Don't under estimate the power in this, just because it is so simple!! You can do it anytime, any place and anywhere, with any issue. . ..and it's free -Wow..... Amazing!

Treat yourself like you would your best friend!

(I said it was easy and simple!) So every time you say something to yourself, like 'my thighs are really fat, my face is full of spots, I'm totally useless at making money', ask yourself if you would say that to your best friend? And I'm guessing that you wouldn't! And that you are about to be shocked, as I was, at how totally *rude* you are to yourself!

Some of the things I have said to myself I wouldn't dream of saying to anyone else!! So why are we saying these horrid, destructive things to ourselves? Do we really expect to feel happy and have a wonderful life when we are condemning ourselves is such an awful way. And ...... If that isn't enough, *(which it is!)*, but how many times a day do we say these things to ourselves? Probably hundreds or even thousands, if we include every single negative comment we think about ourselves, to put ourselves down!

It is seriously time to STOP doing that NOW! How much better are you instantly going to feel if we stop all of this negative programming.

Step 2 - say what you would say to your best friend instead! Don't you deserve to be treated as kindly as you would treat someone else? Yes you do! So try this, I am sure you will be amazed with the results!

The next exercise is a continuation of the above, ie saying good things to ourselves! (& *I have found that if we start each statement or affirmation with our own name then it gives it far more power.*)

So here is the list of statements that I have used on myself, and that I still read, or listen to, as I have recorded most of my releases to help me love myself more and to connect to my true inner self.

Michelle -
I Release Me!

Michelle, I release me now & forever.

Michelle, I deserve to be loved, just the way I am, now and forever.

Michelle, I love you, just the way you are, now and forever.

Michelle, I choose to fill me with love to overflowing, now & forever.

Michelle, I choose to put me first, now.

Michelle, I choose to be my best friend, my true soul mate, now and forever.

Michelle, I love all of me & I feel my love for myself now.

Michelle, I fill myself with total pure love to overflowing now and forever.

Michelle, thank you for choosing to love and accept me, just the way I am, now and forever.

Michelle, I AM proud to be me!

Michelle, I see love & light in my eyes now and always.

Michelle, I see radiance and natural beauty in my face now.

Michelle, I feel I am amazing!

Michelle, I feel that I am my love!!!

Michelle, I love myself in this moment now!

You may well burst into tears whilst reading some of these, if you do then just allow the tears to flow, it is a cleansing and a releasing process and you will feel better for it.

Once you have done this exercise a few times then you will feel better and empowered after reading the statements to yourself, or at least are noticing how much you haven't been loving yourself.

Now the next exercise is a lot more challenging, so only go on to it when you feel ready, and be warned that you may need a box of tissues, if you haven't already.

Yes, it's 'The Mirror Exercise', not for the faint hearted!

(Some of you may benefit from reading *Chapter 15 first, Some Extra Help with Grief and Sadness*)

The Mirror Exercise!

Read the following statements one at a time
then looking into a mirror,
repeat the statement to yourself, looking into your eyes,
Say the statement to yourself with as much love as you can.

(If this proves to be too much or too hard to do, then just read the statements to yourself, slowly, one at a time. When you feel comfortable doing this, try adding looking into the mirror again. You can build up to looking into your eyes, as another step if you need to.

If your self-love is really low, and you find this too hard to do, then you will need a lot of filling up with Divine love through other Divine Transmissions or mixing with high vibrational loving souls, (see my membership group or through My Self-Love audio package - www.

pureloveforever.com) so that you can reach a place of being able to start to love yourself.

Until you reach this place, you won't be fully aware of how much you are not truly loving yourself and that you have been hiding or shielding this fact from yourself, because it has been too painful to face.

When you start to choose to truly love yourself, just as you are now,

then this is the starting point of a new you, filled with love, joy, peace & fun!

Just give it a go,

because **you are worth it and you do deserve it.**

Affirming -
I Love Me!

(Read the following statements looking into your eyes into mirror!)

I am open & receptive to all good.

I release me, now & forever

I deserve to be loved, just the way I am.

I love myself, just the way I am, now & forever

I choose to fill me with love to overflowing, now & forever.

I choose to put me first!

I am my best friend & true soul mate, now & forever.

I love all of me

I (choose to) feel my love for me now

I am total pure love now and forever.

I thank myself for choosing to love & accept me, just the way I am, now & forever.

I am proud to be me!

I see love & light in my eyes

I see radiance & natural beauty in my face now.

I love my body and all the activities it allows me to do.

I feel I am amazing!

I feel that I am my love

I love myself, in this moment of now

Thank you, Thank you, Thank you.

So Who is this NEW ME?

Time for some uplifting questions!

What do I love doing?
What brings me joy and happiness?
What makes me feel excited and alive?

What makes me feel loved?
What makes me feel valued?
What makes me feel special?

What do I do that makes others feel special?
What were my childhood dreams?
If money was no object, what would I choose to do with my life?

Having read lots of self help books in my time, it is probably the done thing to write down all your answers to these questions! And writing does use different parts of the brain and can help you brain-storm! So, if you are struggling with answering the questions, then you may need to do some writing down and brain storming! Maybe take a walk in nature and come back to it, or even better still take your list with you and review it, getting inspiration from nature and your surroundings.

You could also ask (genuine trustworthy) friends for their honest answers to the above questions if you are feeling a bit stuck for some answers, but ultimately the only person who knows the answers to these questions and who is the real me is **you**!

You are the only person who knows the real you

You are the only person who can be the real you

If you have done a really good job at hiding your true, real self from yourself, then you may well need help and guidance from other wise, enlightened people. You will most probably need to do a lot of releasing, there is more information and audio downloads for releasing available on my website at www.pureloveforever.com

But please remember, you have the most important tool of all inside you! The tool to FEEL what is right and what is truth for you.

In finding our 'true self" or 'new me' we need to release all the layers of tissue paper, (layers of bad programming and all the energies that are not ours! And everything that is not a divine truth for us.)

By the way, did you know?

That 98% of all our thoughts and feelings are NOT ours!!

When you next have a negative thought or feeling ask yourself,

'Is this mine?' & feel what you feel for the answer. If you are really empathic, (easily pick up other people's emotions and thoughts then you will benefit from my empathic audios, see my wesbite for details), which I designed so I could live without constantly feeling other people's emotions all the time, which is *so* draining!

So whenever you want to check if something is right for you, is your New You, or is a good path to follow, just:-

Drop into your heart or gut, ask the question, and FEEL the answer!

This is so powerful and so true to you! If you desire to live a happy, loving life, then live through you heart and gut feelings, and leave your thinking to do the finances and technology!!

Trust! Trust! Trust!

Your inner knowing knows all your answers! To fully

Enjoy your life - live through your heart, live in love!

To quote a quote I saw on a lovely inspiring video clip, called 'may you be blessed',

'And when you are tempted to hold back, may you be reminded that Love Flows best when it Flows Freely!'

We do tend to have the bad habit of shutting ourselves down to protect ourselves when life gets challenging! But the best way out of problem is to raise your vibration and Feel Love for the situation. I accept this can be a challenging thing to do, but it is a skill, that with practice can be mastered quite quickly, and the results from using this skill will be profound.

So here are a few tips, things that I do to raise my vibration, when I am feeling challenged, or when you get that kicked in the gut feeling that just knocks all the life and enthusiasm out of you!

Ask Uplifting Questions!

How can I feel happier/ inspired/ full of joy?
What can I do now to feel amazing?
How can I raise my vibration and feel better?
How can I attract an amazing miracle into my life?

Here are some Inspiring Answers and Ideas that I do!

Watch inspiring clips, there are lots of them at <u>www. flickspire.com</u> and you can also find them on You Tube.

Listen to songs that make you feel happy

Watch some funny, light youtube clips! Here are a few of my favourite!

Morecombe & Wise - Bring Me Sunshine
Morecombe & Wise - Singing in the Rain
Kenn Dood - Happiness

Chat with happy, high vibration people (join my membership group!)

Send love! - to someone you love, to someone who is ill, to a hospital, to a country in need, to the whole world! Just send love and you will feel better!

To send love, take a deep breath in, think of where you would like to send the love, (and don't forget to send it to **yourself first**!) then as you slowly release the breath, allow your heart to expand out, keep expanding it out, like a huge ball of sunshine love, radiating love like the sun radiates light. Let your love grow and grow until it shines into the whole of the world!

The more love we all radiate into the world the easier it will be for us to connect to love and feel happy and loved all the time.

We all have the power to change the world! Just one thought and one smile at a time! Share *your love and your smile* with everyone you meet, and see how much better you feel and how many smiles you get back.

SO..... Who is the new you?

Someone who wants to change the world, one thought and one smile at a time?

I truly trust and hope so!

Sending you all lots of LOVE from my big shining, Love Sun, from my Heart!

Getting Rid
of Layers!

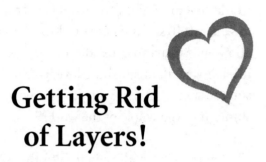

How do we get rid of layers?

Well there are many ways and methods being used by various energy healers in the world today, but here are the ones that have worked best for me.

The first one we have already talked about, 'asking is this mine?'

As already noted earlier in the book, 98% of all thoughts, beliefs and feelings we have aren't even ours! So this seems like a good starting place - get rid of the 98% that doesn't belong to you and then the remaining 2% will be so much easier!

I find releasing is an amazingly incredible and powerful way to get rid of unwanted feelings, emotions, beliefs, programs, and in fact all unwanted, impure energies from our energy field.

So, how do I do it, you may be asking?

To release something, you just simply say to yourself 'I release all energies relating to ......' eg if you wish to release your feelings about a conversation you've just had with someone that has left you feeling upset or angry, then you would say, 'I release all upset, anger and other energies relating to the conversation with .....'

Yes - it IS that simple!! Of course, you can go in to it on a much deeper level for big core beliefs etc, but for now, let's just stick to the easy and simple and how to get started!

So important guidelines - Drink lots of water, during and after releasing. This is the advice that all holistic therapists give to their clients, as we are 90% water, we need to keep the water moving inside our bodies to flush all the toxins out, which are physically brought to the surface to physically release by the releasing statement.

You may feel a physical sensation when releasing or after a release, often a feeling of 'energy' rising and a feeling of being lighter. For larger issues you could feel a headache, (drink more water) or release through yawning, hiccups or even a muscle spasm, so they are all normal!

When we do a release, then energy moves out of our energy field, leaving a space. This space can then be filled with a different energy. Often, our sub-conscious mind will look for the energy that we have released to be back in the pattern that it is used to, so I like to fill 'all space released with pure love' at the end of any release, so that nothing unwanted can float into your new space! I also send all energy releasing back to source, because it is low vibration and negative energy, so no one else wants to take it on board either!

So a simple example,

I release all thoughts, feelings and emotions affecting me now that are not mine,

I release all energies and low vibrations from the whole of my mind, body, spirit and energy field, from this moment of now.

I fill the whole of myself, all energy being released and all space created to overflowing with Pure Love, Light and Peace, Now and Forever.

Even though the above example is very simply phrased, it is still incredibly powerful, to release all thoughts, emotions & energies etc that are not yours is huge! For this reason, I have intentionally only written to release them from this moment of now. You can release from future moments of now and across time, space, dimension and realities, but I would recommend that you do the above one several times and reach a point of 'no more releasing', before you add any additional statements to it!

Please remember:-

Please drink lots of water whilst releasing and afterwards for several days to keep the energy flowing through your body and out of your energy system. (In fact, please drink water every day!!) How quickly will water flow through a dried up sponge as to a wet one? It is the same with energy and water in our bodies, if we want everything to work and flow well then we need to keep it hydrated!

Releasing can also be used for more in depth issues. However, most of our deepest core beliefs and issues have so much energy attached to them that they do need a higher energy to release them.* This is why so many people seek the services and tools of Energy Healers. It feels safer for them and the Energy Healer is able, with their higher vibration, to release energies that would remain to heavy for the individual to release on their own at that time. They are also able to uncover issues that have been well hidden in the layers of tissue paper, maybe for many years and lifetimes, and to release these hidden layers.

Releasing advice and help is available from me, please visit my website: www.pureloveforever.com for more details.

- *Einstein stated that a problem cannot be changed with the same level of energy that created it, ie you need a higher vibration to release a problem than the vibration that created it. If you raise your own vibration to a level higher than when the problem was created then you can release the issue yourself. If you cannot raise you vibration high enough on your own, then you will need help to do this or have the issue released for you.*
- (Not the exact quote, but my simple interpretation of it)

You Have the Power to Change the World!

Yea, right! I can hear you all saying! That's for people who are better than me, I'm just not good enough to do that, or I'd love to be able to change the world, but I'm just me, and I just don't know how I could possibly make a difference!

So, I am going to give you several ways that are simple and easy to do that anyone can do *each day*!

Are you ready?

How do you *feel* when someone smiles at you?
How do you *feel* when someone gives you a compliment?
How do you *feel* when someone encourages and supports you?

Well, I know that I feel good, and so do all the people that I have interacted with, so I am assuming that you also feel good for all of the above questions!

So that means that the person or people who did the above things raised your vibration from where it was to a higher vibration of happiness!

And that means that if YOU were to:-

Smile at someone
Give someone a compliment
Encourage or support someone

Then you will have raised their vibration to a higher vibration of happiness!

If that person then repeats these actions with another person, then you have raised the vibration of one person and indirectly assisted to raise the vibration of another person! Cool work!!

And here we have the effects of the chain reaction. So over the course of a day, how many people's vibrations can you raise, either directly or indirectly?

This is where the power to change the world comes from. The collected small acts of kindness that each one of us can do, at the end of a day all add up to a big raise in vibration, or collective consciousness, as I believe it is called.

The truth is, we don't actually know how big a difference we make in the world. We have no idea how much we may touch someone's heart and soul in that moment. We have no idea that someone might be so low and desperate that they are thinking of ending their lives, and then we smile at them, or say 'I love your pretty dress' etc and they feel a wave of love and appreciation and think that maybe life is worth another chance. (I have heard stories of just this happening.) So,

WE ALL DO HAVE THE POWER TO MAKE A DIFFERENCE.

The question is, are we willing to choose to make a difference?

Most of us have computers, access to emails, facebook, twitter and so on. So how do we use these forms of communication? Do we use them to inspire and help others? Or do we use them to gossip and be unkind?

The same principle applies to everything we do, whether in person, on the phone, through a computer or internet and even through our thoughts!

Yes, thoughts have power!

Which aptly brings us to our next chapter, which has just been renamed by that last thought and the statement I have just written!!

Thoughts have Power!

Life can be complicated and it can sometimes be difficult with all the influences there are going on around us, to follow our true paths, be our true selves and know what will allow our diamond to sparkle and what won't, so I thought it would be a good idea to simplify 'life' for us!

All in favour shout 'I'! - So pleased you all agree, well the majority of you! So here we go.

Basically, there are just two emotions – 'Love & Fear', every other emotion we feel is a sub-emotion of one of these. So in any given moment, all we have to do is ask, what am I feeling 'love' or 'fear'? Now, how simple is that! And I can hear some oh buts coming up, but it can be that simple if we choose and allow it to be that simple!!

So let's expand this idea, to fully understand it, then we can collapse it back in to simple, easy, just need to choose to do it concept / action!

Emotions of Love

Happy, joyous, inspired, loving, caring, sharing, giving, fun, laughter, confidence, self belief, inner knowing, appreciation, gratitude, trust, etc

Emotions of Fear

Anger, frustration, jealousy, insecurity, hate, failure, despair, depression, grief, sadness, being controlled, manipulation, etc

Now all emotions of fear can be released. I'm going to write that again!

ALL EMOTIONS OF FEAR CAN BE RELEASED!

'I release all emotions, feelings, thoughts and energies of (anger, jealousy, hate, grief, sadness etc) from the whole of my mind, body, spirit and energy field, in this moment of now (& all future moments of now)'

Just like that - so simple!

Of course, you need to specify which emotion is causing your fear, and you may need to say the release several times, over several days, or even weeks or months, if it is a deep rooted fear.

But. *all emotions of fear can be released*!

So we have no excuse or reason to choose fear! And if we look more closely at the reasons why we do or have been allowing fear to influence us and the effect this can have on others, then may be that will inspire and motivate us **to choose to release the fear and choose love instead.**

The Chain of Kindness

When someone hurts or upsets us our immediate reaction, is to either hurt them back or retreat and protect ourselves. Both of these reactions will bring us further upset and hurt. Obviously, we all know that two wrongs don't make a right, and adding bad to bad just makes more bad! And shutting ourselves off to protect ourselves is just stopping the flow of love, which is cutting us off from the very thing we most desire, love and to be loved, seen, appreciated and valued. Who is going to give us all these feelings if we dam up our flow of love?

So when someone hurts us, this is the time when we most need to connect to love, feel love, keep our love flowing and **love ourselves**!

Usually the act that upset us, was done because the person who sent it out was feeling unloved, unwanted, undeserving and was crying out for some attention and love for them! Imagine how different the chain of reactions would be if we all responded with **love**, each and every time someone upset and hurt us! If we could see their action as a shout for help, life is tough for me now and I don't know how to deal with it', or 'will someone please be nice to me and help me out of this black hole!' then it would be easier to react in a more loving way.

We all have the power to change a 'chain of reaction' each time we interact with someone.

If someone shares a chain of kindness with us then we usually and without thinking carry on that chain of kindness.

Unfortunately, it is often also true that when a 'chain of unkindness' shows itself to us, that we pass on the unkindness to some other unsuspecting person!

We all have the power to stop and break every chain of unkindness that we come across, with a simple comment such as, 'I'm sorry you feel that way, are you having a bad day', 'can I do anything to help you?' Or 'I'm sorry you are feeling like that', 'I do hope your day improves'. Any positive comment, or acknowledgment of their feelings, takes away the hurt we could take on.

It is their issue, that they are struggling to deal with, and us accepting their emotional upset, does nothing to help us, them or the rest of the world! Let's all make a conscious effort to change every chain of unkindness into a chain of kindness, every time we come across one. We won't always remember or succeed, but every time we do, we have changed the world into a happier place!

Feel proud of all the efforts you are doing and don't beat yourself up for the odd times when you don't get the result you desired!

Every little step, thought, smile you do makes a difference, and that is what counts. Avoid focusing on the negative.

WE GIVE POWER TO WHATEVER WE CHOOSE TO THINK.

So even if you are disappointed or annoyed with yourself, be kind to yourself, as you would your best friend and acknowledge that you are doing your best 'at this moment of time, with your current level of knowledge and junk!' When you have a better understanding of life, love, energy and releasing and less junk then it will be easier to always choose Love.

I am hoping and trusting that you all now see the power we have to either positively or negatively influence others around us, just as outside influences have the power to influence us, if we are not aware of this and are not actively choosing to stop this from happening.

I am also trusting that as you have read this far, that you are now choosing to choose love!

So next chapter coming up, again just been renamed by that thought!

Help with choosing to choose love!

Help with Choosing to Choose Love!

Having discovered and accepted that every thought and emotion either comes from Love or Fear, then to choose Love and release the fear, we need to know exactly what the fear is.

For releasing to be effective we do need to be specific. Asking for all fears to be released is really too big a job to be processed. The more we can break down the release into specific little releases then the more effective they will be.

So how do we find out what the fear really is, as quite often the fear is hidden and not the obvious at all?

I find the easiest way to answer a question is to ask more questions! But they do need to be inspiring questions that will lead to a desired answer!

So, some good questions to ask would be:-

How exactly do I feel?
How often do I feel like this?
Is this feeling associated with a certain person / people / place / activity?
Is this a really strong feeling?
Is this feeling mine?

Once you have more information on the fear then you can do a release to get rid of this fear, so next time you stumble into it you won't react in the same way.

So here are a few examples to help you get investigating and releasing any fears showing their ugly heads!

'I release all fears of being manipulated and being talked into doing something that I don't' want to do, from the whole of my mind, body, spirit and energy field and fill with Divine Love, Peace & Truth.'

'I release all feelings of not being good enough and being a failure from the whole of my being and fill with Divine Love, Light, Peace & Joy.'

'I release all feelings of anger relating to being walked all over by others and all frustration and annoyance towards myself for allowing this to happen, and fill with Divine Love, Light, Peace & Joy.'

Some Extra Advice and Love for Grief and Sadness

Life can be extremely tough when we are going through a period of grief and sadness. It can seem never ending, and like there is no answer or cure. It may feel like it is a challenge that has taken us one step too far and we cannot cope with it anymore and just want someone to wave a magic wand and make it all go away.

Well, I am truly trusting that the following information will be a magic wand for you. To fully recover from any grief or sadness, we need to understand what has happened in terms of energy, so that we can use the most appropriate method to release the trapped grief and sadness from inside us.

If we go back to Our Diamond story, this will give a good visual example and hopefully help you realize why you are struggling so much with recovering from your grief. When you suffer an incident that causes you grief, (from losing a loved one, a pet, a miscarriage, or even a home you loved or a treasured possession), this loss wraps us in layers of tissue paper. The deeper the loss, the more layers of tissue paper are added and the darker the colour is. So if we suddenly have 3 or 4 layers of black tissue paper wrapped around our diamond, then we feel totally disconnected from ourselves, our shining light and our inner power and knowing. We will feel isolated, because we have lost sight and feeling of who we are and the energy that makes us feel good. Our vibration instantly drops to an all time low and we just cannot manage to raise it with all the usual methods. This leads to despair that life is always going to be this bad, which lowers our vibration even more.

However, all of this is not the case and is not a truth at all. The layers of grief and sadness can be released the same as any other layer of unwanted energy we have wrapped around our diamond.

For those of you who have reached the point, that I am so fed up with crying all the time, and are probably working really hard not to cry, then please listen carefully and take on board this next piece of advice.

Often when we release energy from our bodies, there is a physical reaction in the body, which is the trapped energy actually physically releasing from our bodies, and this is a really good thing, it shows that the releasing is working! Physical reactions can vary from coughing, sneezing, yawning, burping, headaches, muscle spasms, laughing and crying. From my experience, grief and sadness are released through crying, which can cause a catch 22 situation, as we want to feel happy, so we try not to cry and in stopping ourselves from crying we are actually preventing the trapped emotions from releasing. So, we need to look at our views of crying and change those views, so we can allow ourselves to release all the hurt and sadness from the whole of our bodies and feel well and happy again.

What if crying wasn't actually a sad emotion? What if it was just a process of releasing a sad emotion. ie it's not part of the emotion, it is part of the release. This would then mean that crying is a physical sign that we are releasing all our hurt and upset, which is good, so we should be pleased that we have cried!

Now, I accept this is totally weird and not want you expected to hear, but have any of the traditional views worked for you so far?

One of the most beautiful descriptions I've heard for expressing crying was:-

Tears cleanse your soul.

So what if tears dissolve all the black tissue paper that is keeping you disconnected from your shining light, inner self and feeling your happiness. And what if we could release some of the pain and hurt from the tears and crying, so that we can cry without feeling all of the sadness.

So here is a release that I have specially written to do just this, so you can feel safe and accepting that it is good for you to cry and that it is an important part of your releasing process. The more you take this on board, the more tears you can release in one go, and the fewer sessions of crying you will have and the quicker you will feel HAPPY again!

'I release all thoughts, feelings and beliefs that I should not keep crying and that crying is weak or unacceptable behaviour,

I release the feelings of deep hurt, sadness and grief from my crying, so the tears can flow freely and these emotions can easily be released,

I fill to overflowing, all energies released, all space created and the whole of my being, with pure love and light, and pure self-love, support and understanding, now and forever.'

I would recommend that you work with the above release, until you can read it without tears, before you progress onto the next release. (You can of course do both together, but be prepared for a massive release of tears, which is fine and possibly even a good thing to do, if you are ready to just get it all out. Only you can decide which is most appropriate for you.

I send you pure love to overflowing, and ask you to know and always remember that this is just a process and you will feel happy again.

'I release all emotions of grief, sadness and hurt from the whole of my mind, body, spirit and energy field, from this moment of now and all future moments of now.

I fill to overflowing, all energies released, all space created and the whole of my being, with pure love and light, and pure self-love, support and understanding, now and forever.'

Releases to Help You

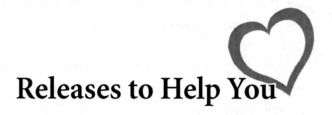

A Morning Release to Start Your Day

'I release all energies that are less than love,
& all energies that may stop my day being an amazing,
happy day, full of wonderful miracles and surprises,
Blue skies and happy smiling faces!

I Fill the whole of me and the whole of my day and everyone
I meet, with pure love, light, fun and joy.
I fill my day with miracles and joyous surprises.
I love my life and I love me!'

An Evening Release to Sleep Well

'I release all energies that have entered my mind, body,
spirit or energy field today that are not mine,

I release all thoughts, feelings, emotions and low vibrations from the whole of me from this moment of now and all future moments of now,

I release all vibrations and energies that are in my mind now and fill my mind with complete stillness, love, harmony and peace.

I release any energies that are preventing me from sleeping peacefully and soundly, and awaking fully healed, recharged and full of vitality and enthusiasm for a brand new amazing day!

I fill the whole of my being and energy field with pure love, stillness, peace and harmony, now and forever.'

A Release for Moments of Worry & Fear

'I release all thoughts, feeling, emotions and low vibrations that are not mine,

I release everything and all energies that are not me,

I release all thoughts, low vibrations and energies that are causing me worry or upset now,

I release all of these from the whole of my mind, body, spirit and energy field, from this moment of now and all future moments of now, across eternal time, space, dimension and realities, now and forever.

I fill the whole of myself, my being, my energy field, all energies released and all space created to overflowing, with pure divine love, light and peace now and forever.'

A Release for Not Feeling Love

'I release all thoughts, feelings, emotions, low vibrations and energies that are stopping me from feeling love now,

I release all energies that are preventing me from feeling my true self and connecting to my shining, bright diamond,

I release all energies that are stopping me from choosing love, living in love and spreading love to others,

I fill the whole of myself, my being, my energy field, all energies released and all space created to overflowing, with pure divine love, light and peace now and forever.'

A Release for Not Feeling Good Enough

'I release all thoughts, feelings, emotions, low vibrations and energies that are causing me to feel not good enough and to not value myself now,

I release all energies that are preventing me from seeing, feeling, acknowledging and knowing that I am worthy, I am deserving and I am good enough, NOW, just the way I am.

I release all energies that are stopping me from loving myself and being kind to myself, and from treating myself as well as I would a best friend,

I fill the whole of myself, my being, my energy field, all energies released and all space created to overflowing, with pure divine love, light and peace now and forever.'

A Release for a Boost of Energy!

'I release all energies and low vibrations that are draining me and preventing me from feeling full of life, vitality and enthusiasm for whatever I am choosing to do now,

I release all thoughts, feelings, emotions and beliefs that are preventing me from connecting to my true self now, and my inner power and guidance.

I release all energies that are stopping me from taking a few minutes to just 'appreciate me, just as I am, in this moment of now', and all the efforts I am putting into all I do.

I fill the whole of myself and my energy field, to overflowing, with pure love, light, peace, harmony, joy and love for me.

I thank myself and the universe for all I have and all the love and joy I can see, hear, touch, taste and feel in my life every day.'

The End! - Or Should I Say 'Your Start!'

This is 'The End' of my book.

But you can read it again, as many times as you like and I really do send out the thought that you do, as each time you read it, you will read and hear different things from the words, as your energy and understanding changes. So please do keep this book handy and in view, to remind you to re-read it every month or so to evaluate your progress and take your understanding to the next level.

Both the words, intentions and even the cover of this book have been 'Infused and Filled with Divine Energies' so just reading, looking at or holding this book will release unwanted energies for you and raise your vibration.

Also we do forget to do many of the things that we know will help to make our lives smoother and easier. Each time I re-read this book, I am also reminded – 'oh I should really do that more!' and I work with energy and helping people every day and teaching these principles!

I am hoping and trusting that this book has given you enough help, advice and insight to start living a:-

Brand New Life and Being a Brand New You!

Anytime, you feel unsure of what to do or what to choose then remember to keep it simple!

Just ask yourself, is this *Love or Fear*?

If it's Love then go with it!

If it's fear then release it!!

If you don't know or aren't sure than ask your heart or gut for confirmation.

If in doubt, do nothing until the answer becomes clear.

TRUST! TRUST! & TRUST!

Please remember:-

We **all** do have the power to make a difference.

The question is are we willing to choose to make a difference?

- ♥ Choose to live in love
- ♥ Choose the chain of kindness
- ♥ Choose to make the world a better, happier place for us all to live in, just one thought and one smile at a time.

There is an amazing group of like minded people in my membership group – all working to raise their vibrations and live in love and make the world a happier place for us all to live in, so we would love you to join us!

http://www.pureloveforever.com

Thank you for reading my book.

Sending love and blessings to you all.

Lightning Source UK Ltd.
Milton Keynes UK
UKOW04f1014161014

240184UK00002B/6/P